**Exploring Markets**

Stefan Kühl is professor of sociology at the University of Bielefeld in Germany and works as a consultant for Metaplan, a consulting firm based in Princeton, Hamburg, Shanghai, Singapore, Versailles and Zurich. He studied sociology and history at the University of Bielefeld (Germany), Johns Hopkins University in Baltimore (USA), Université Paris-X-Nanterre (France) and the University of Oxford (UK).

Other Books by Stefan Kühl

*Organizations: A Systems Approach*
(Routledge 2013)
*Ordinary Organizations: Why Normal Men Carried Out the Holocaust*
(Polity Press 2016)
*When the Monkeys Run the Zoo: The Pitfalls of Flat Hierarchies*
(forthcoming)
*Sisyphus in Management: The Futile Search for the Optimal Organizational Structure*
(forthcoming)
*The Rainmaker Effect: Contradictions of the Learning Organization*
(forthcoming)


To contact us:
Metaplan
101 Wall Street
Princeton, NJ 08540
USA
Phone: +1 609-688-9171
stefankuehl@metaplan.com
www.metaplan.com

Stefan Kühl

# Exploring Markets

A Very Brief Introduction

Organizational Dialogue Press
Princeton, Hamburg, Shanghai, Singapore, Versailles, Zurich

ISBN (Print) 978-0-9991479-4-8
ISBN (EPUB) 978-0-9991479-5-5

Copyright © 2017 by Stefan Kühl

All rights reserved. No part of this publication may be reproduced or transmitted in any form or by any means, without permission in writing from the author.

Translated by: Adam Blauhut
Cover Design: Guido Klütsch
Typesetting: Thomas Auer
Project Management: Tabea Koepp
www.organizationaldialoguepress.com

# Contents

Foreword:
Market Exploration Instead of Market Research ..................... 7

1.
Observing the Environment ................................................................. 12

   1.1 An Organization's Environment ............................................... 12
   1.2. Alignment with Similar Organizations in the Same Field ............. 15

2.
Beyond the Objectivist View—the Cognitive Turn .............. 21

   2.1. The Objectivist View of the World ......................................... 21
   2.2 "Forming"—How Organizations Create
       Their View of the Environment ............................................... 25
   2.3 The Diversity and Narrowing
       of Perspectives in Organizations .............................................. 32

## 3.
## Approaches to Exploration ..................................................................42

    3.1. Re-Framing—Changing the Organization's View
        of the Environment....................................................................43

    3.2. "De-Generalization" of Statements .......................................49

    3.3. Hypotheses Formation—Articulating Assumptions
        in Order to Make Progress with Exploration ....................53

## 4.
## Options for Constructing Reality—Conclusion......................54

## Bibliography..........................................................................................57

# Foreword: Market Exploration Instead of Market Research

The title of this book, "Exploring Markets," does not accurately reflect its content. The book focuses not only on how businesses view their product markets, labor markets and financial markets, but, more generally, on how different types of organizations perceive their environment and justify decisions on the basis of their perceptions. Even if market research approaches tend to reduce discussions about organizational alignment with a relevant section of the environment to businesses, we should not ignore the way other types of organizations observe their environment. After all, it is often more difficult for public administrations, armies, political parties, government departments, hospitals and universities to take in their complex environments than it is for companies.

The title "Exploring Markets" is likely to confuse many readers, since the verb "to explore" typically calls to mind groups of schoolchildren exploring the natural environment on an excursion or ten-month-old infants consciously registering their immediate environment for the first time. However, even though this book is concerned with how companies perceive their environment in general and thus moves beyond the exploration of markets, we decided to keep the title.

We have chosen the word "exploring" quite deliberately. The more common term, "researching markets," stands for an approach that continues to dominate organizational practice today, one that assumes that an organization's environment can be determined "objectively." The work performed at most market research institutes and departments is characterized by the idea that these institutes and departments can grasp market developments as they "really" are if only they collect data according to scientific standards of reliability, validity and representativeness. This notion reflects the instrumental-rational understanding of organizations that long dominated management circles in the past and is based on the assumption that organizations can derive the right strategies—i.e., the means to achieve a purpose or aim—from a precise analysis of the environment and then construct an entire organization based on means-ends chains.

By using the term "exploring markets," we signal that we reject the notion that markets can be investigated objectively. With the cognitive turn in organizational science, researchers came to recognize that an organization's structure plays a key role in determining its view of its environment. If different views exist within an organization—so goes the thinking—it has nothing to do with the fact that the single "proper" view has not yet established itself, but rather with the fact that the individual organizational units are integrated into the organizational structure in different ways and perceive their environment through individual observation grids.

The aim of this booklet is to show what form market exploration can take beyond this relatively narrow perspective. The first chapter illustrates how organizations observe their environments and to what extent they take their cue from other organizations in their organizational field. The second chapter explains why the long-dominant theory that organizations can objectively grasp their environment is insufficient. In contrast to this theory, we demonstrate that organizations construct their environment themselves. The third chapter offers a detailed description of how organizations can selectively change the way they perceive their environment through the techniques of de-generalization and hypothesis formation. Nevertheless, there is only one way to fundamentally change perceptions of the environment and that is to change organizational structure. The fourth chapter—our summary—briefly discusses how this can be done.

I have written this book mainly for practitioners in companies, public administrations, hospitals, schools, armies, police departments, political parties and associations. When describing the approach, I draw on our many years of experience in helping companies, public administrations, universities, hospitals and non-profit organizations explore their environments. I constantly show in individual passages where the approach we promote incorporates elements from current market research practices and where it deviates from them.

Even though this book was written for real-world application based on real-world experience, our goal is to ensure that the reflections it introduces are aligned with modern approaches in organizational theory. Without disregarding the fundamentally different lines of thought and application contexts in organizational theory, on the one hand, and organizational practice, on the other, I aim to present a proven approach that does not immediately elicit a pitying smile from an organizational scientist because of its allegedly simplistic understanding of organizations. In a number of passages—e.g. when developing the "forming" concept to explain an organization's perceptions of its environment—I even aspire to go beyond current research.

This book is part of a series in which we provide organizational practitioners with the essentials of a key management topic against the backdrop of modern organizational theory. In addition to this volume, *Exploring Markets*, we will also publish books on the topics of *Designing Organizations, Influencing Organizational Culture, Developing Mission Statements, Managing Projects, Developing Strategies,* and *Lateral Leadership*. These books can be read individually if practitioners wish to learn about a specific problem within their organizations. On the other hand, they have been conceived as a series to ensure that, when they are read, they produce a consistent, coherent view of the functionality of organizations and the options practitioners have to influence them. Because they have been cast from the same mold, attentive readers will constantly find related lines of thought and similar phrases in all the books. These overlaps are intentional and are included to emphasize the consistency of the underlying construct of ideas and the many links between the different guides.

We do not believe in simplifying texts for managers and consultants through bullet points, executive summaries, text-flow diagrams, or practice exercises. In most cases these aids infantilize readers because they are based on the assumption that readers are unable to identify the central ideas of the text themselves without additional assistance. For this reason, in addition to a few, sparingly used graphics, we employ only a single element (as in all the other *Management Compact* guides) to make the book easier to read. In small boxes we give examples not only to flesh out our thoughts but also to show more in-depth connections to organizational theory. Readers who are pressed for time or are uninterested in these topics can skip the boxes without losing track of the general thread of the book.

Initial reflections on how organizations construct their environments can be found in my books *The Rainmaker Effect: Contradictions of the Learning Organization* and *Sisyphus in Management: The Futile Search for the Optimal Organizational Structure*. Readers who are interested in understanding the organizational structure through which organizations construct environmental perceptions are referred to the publication *Organizations: A Systems Approach* (Kühl 2013). Here, for the first time, I develop the nine-field matrix for assessing organizational structure, which is crucial for understanding the organization's different perspectives on its environment.

This book was developed as part of Metaplan's training program "Leadership and Consulting through Discourse." We would like to thank the program participants not only for critically questioning the approach we aim to introduce here, but also for sharing their practical experiences and diverse input. Special thanks also goes to the many organizational scientists who have critically reflected on and discussed Metaplan's work over the last few decades.

# 1.
# Observing the Environment

Every organization needs to gather information about its environment. Companies need to get an impression of what their customers want, which strategies their competitors are employing and how political regulations are changing. Government departments need to adapt to the different ways organizations respond to their laws and regulations as well as to the different responses these laws and regulations trigger among lobbying organizations. Political parties need to understand what makes their potential voters tick and how they are viewed in relation to other parties.

But what exactly is an organization's "environment"? How does this environment evolve and what mechanisms do organizations use to observe their environment?

## 1.1 An Organization's Environment

Whether they take the form of groups, families, movements or organizations, systems describe everything they cannot attribute to themselves as their environment. For a gang of teenagers hanging out at the street corner, the environment can be a rival gang hanging out at the next street corner. For families, it can be the school where their children are educated. For social movements, it can be the policy, economic system or branch of science that they are protesting. For organizations, it can be the customers to which they want to sell their products and services.

But it is possible that the environment defined by a system does not see itself as this system's environment. As Niklas Luhmann observed, a company might imagine that it has "customers," even though the people thus described would hardly "label themselves or even want to be addressed" as customers of this particular company. Porsche drivers, owners of luxury cell phones and purchasers of prestigious designer handbags who define their identities based on their role as consumers are the exception that proves the rule (Luhmann 2000, 239).

What an organization attributes to its environment and what it attributes to itself is often quite arbitrary. Oil companies can operate gas stations on their own. If this is the case, the buildings and the equipment belong to the oil company, it hires the workers and it records the income and expenses in its books. However, it can also have independent tenants operate the service stations. Even if the oil company can contractually require the tenants to purchase, at inflated prices, a specified quantity of its own gas and its own products for the gas station shop, the oil company nevertheless represents the environment of the gas station (seen here as an organization itself) or a part of this environment. If, in response to pressure from the oil company, a tenant operates just within or even outside the bounds of the law by employing workers off the books or remaining open longer than mandatory closing times, the oil companies can always claim they have nothing to do with it.

Like all other systems, organizations have no choice but to observe only a part of their environment because this environment is far more complex than the systems themselves. And because every organization needs to cope with the complexity of its environment, it has no choice but to work with simplifications and omissions when observing its environment (Luhmann 1995, 181ff.). In this way, like all other systems, organizations convince themselves of the relevance of only a very small cross-section of what is theoretically part of their environment. The rest is just noise to them. An ice cream company views, as its environment, the purchasers of its products, the suppliers of raw materials, the logistics companies that transport its goods, as well as its competitors—but not necessarily an army of children fighting in East Congo, a Russian expedition to the Antarctic or members of a movement protesting unaffordable housing in Israel.

It is often arbitrary which parts of the environment are perceived by organizations. Sometimes new employees, due to their previous professional activities, bring fresh perspectives to the organization that were not considered relevant before. Sometimes, to everyone's surprise, the introduction of new communication channels leads to new aspects of the environment becoming suddenly relevant to the organization. There is an aspect of uncertainty, relativity, even arbitrariness surrounding the simplifications and omissions made by organizations when observing their environment.

Especially over the last century, organizations have developed a variety of mechanisms to help them grasp their environment in a more systematic way. At some point, companies began methodically studying market and consumer research, employing trend researchers and performing competitor analysis. Associations were formed to monitor political changes and to communicate these changes in an easily comprehensible form to member organizations in the business world, the academic community, the mass media and the healthcare system. Political parties began commissioning polling companies to determine their voters' opinions and to learn how they could best distinguish themselves from other parties. Under the heading of quality management, even public administrations, universities and prisons began measuring "customer" satisfaction.

The background was that organizations had increasingly gained the impression that their environment had become a black box whose content was largely unknown. In their opinion, between what they produced and what their environment was willing to purchase, there existed "gulfs," "divides" and even "mountains" that they could only overcome with the help of "guides" and "scouts."

## 1.2. Alignment with Similar Organizations in the Same Field

Individuals play an important role in many organizations' environments. Hospitals, for example, do not treat families, groups of people or organizations, but individual patients. As a rule, in an election, political parties receive votes not from organized groups of voters or from families, but from individual voters. And in most cases, companies sell their products and services not to groups, families or protest movements, but to individual customers.

Often, though, the environment observed by organizations consists primarily of other organizations. Organizational fields (previously called "organizational sets") emerge when organizations exchange information, concepts, people, services and goods (for more on early approaches to determining organizational fields, see Evan 1966, 318ff.). Organizations adapt to their environment by engaging in such exchanges or simply by observing other organizations that are relevant to them. In many cases, such adaptation processes are reinforced by the fact that organizations in the same field are dependent on professional organizations such as medical and bar associations or on regulatory authorities (see DiMaggio/Powell 1983, 148f.).

Organizations in the same organizational field can be similar—for example, they may produce the same product or compete in the same market. But they can also differ in quite significant ways. One example is an IT firm that caters to the banking industry. Although it might not resemble banks in terms of its structure, it nevertheless helps shape the industry in which banks operate. Another example is regulatory authorities in the pharmaceutical industry. Their main point of reference is the government, but they nevertheless influence the organizational field of pharmaceutical companies, which is more heavily geared toward the private economy.

Traditional market research literature is based on the assumption that, when developing new products or services, organizations are guided by end user needs. The premise is that companies "explore" their customers' needs and tailor their product innovations to them. Political parties listen to their constituencies and modify their platforms in response to the feedback.

However, organizational research has shown that when observing the environment, many organizations are not guided by the market, but by competitors in the same organizational field (see White 1981, 517ff.). We know from studies on sectors as diverse as the hospitality industry (Lant/Baum 1995), mechanical engineering (Heidenreich/Schmidt 1992) and development aid (Kühl 2009) that innovations are not usually the result of changing customer requirements, but of observing competitors.

One example is pricing. According to economic theory, the pricing of a service needs to be based on what a customer is willing to pay for it, and companies must therefore find out just how interested customers are in a product. Only in the rarest of cases, though, do companies set prices by systematically analyzing supply and demand. In a study of American industry, for example, Robert Hall (2002) found that, surprisingly enough, there was not necessarily a correlation between an increase in demand, on the one hand, and a rise in prices, on the other. His finding suggests that price formation usually takes place independently of a specific demand. Until pirating became rampant, the recording industry, for example, assumed that the price of CDs was largely irrelevant to customers and that it thus made no difference whether a CD cost 12 or 17 dollars.

Financial crises show at regular intervals that in many cases banks base their loan decisions not on a detailed review of customer creditworthiness, but on whether other banks have lent money to the same customers. In a discussion among Austrian bank managers on the reasons for the excessive debt levels of the Coop Group, for example, it became clear that, when awarding loans, banks had focused only on which other banks had granted loans to the group. These banks not only abandoned their own review process, but also overlooked the institutions that had refused to grant loans (see Luhmann 1991, 191). The 2008 financial crisis, triggered by the collapse of the American subprime mortgage market, also illustrates what can happen when banks take their cue from the lending practices of other banks when assessing creditworthiness (see Varoufakis 2012, 176ff.).

### EXAMPLE

#### Focusing on Competitors, Not Customers—Lateral Leadership as an Example

The launch of a seminar on lateral leadership provides a case study of the focus on an organizational field. Ten years ago, the consulting firm that developed this management concept was the only provider of seminars dealing with it, but just a few years later, a total of fifteen German consulting and continuing education institutes offered lateral leadership programs.

It is interesting to note that the number of seminars on lateral leadership mushroomed even though the developers of the concept did not earn any money from it for a long time. The seminar concept was kept in the original firm's education program for several years, although it initially did not pay off. A number of other effects were considered to be more important, including the fact that the firm's consultants could be trained in the set of instruments when they taught the seminar, and the company's reputation was enhanced because it was able to offer seminars dealing specifically with organization analysis. These non-monetary factors, of which competitors were unaware, led these competitors to copy the seemingly lucrative management concept, even though there was not sufficient demand for the seminars.

The proliferation of the seminars had the paradoxical effect that demand increased as the seminars began paying off (although this was not the original firm's intention). Due to the diverse seminars on lateral leadership, the media outlets that targeted consultants, trainers and providers of continuing education courses assumed that the topic was a new trend. They published articles confirming that "lateral leadership is just now taking off in the continuing education sector." Not only did this type of media coverage lead to a growing number of consultants, trainers and continuing education providers participating in the seminars, but staff development specialists at companies, public administrations and hospitals also felt compelled to integrate the topic into their seminar programs.

This focus on competitors rather than on customers is functional. For service providers, it is often difficult to satisfy customer requirements because the related information is not readily available. Worse still, customers often do not know exactly what they want themselves. Competitors, on the other hand, are much easier to observe and read. Whereas a customer's ideas about a product are often rather vague, the products sold by the competition are transparent. Whereas customers are often unaware of the price they are willing to pay for a product, it is easy to find out the competitors' prices. Expressed in the language of systems theory, we can say that the more complex an environment is, the more organizations focus on observing other market participants (Luhmann 1990, 191).

# 2.
# Beyond the Objectivist View— the Cognitive Turn

As human beings, we tend to believe that there is one "proper," "objective" view of the environment. After all, to armchair philosophers, "a table is just a table"—this is a fact that no one can deny. We recognize it as a table by its four legs or by the table top and it is no accident that we all agree it is a table. If a person is unable to recognize a table, they either come from a country where there are no tables or they should make an appointment with an eye doctor or a psychiatrist.

Members of organizations also believe that there is a proper, objective view of their environment. Their aim is thus to discover the things that are "out there" already and ultimately waiting to be discovered (see Smircich/Stubbart 1985, 725f.).

## 2.1. The Objectivist View of the World

In many organizations, people are convinced that they can gain an objective understanding of their environment if only they use the right tools. It is assumed, for example, that market research is a proven approach based on scientific methods and that it can be used to "correctly" grasp an organization's environment. "Through market research," writes Karl Suthoff (1960, 87), economists are given a tool with which they can "conduct behavioral research and shed light on increasingly complex markets."

In most respects, the traditional market research approach resembles the prevailing methodology in empirical social research. The study design must reflect the problem at hand, a data collecting method must be defined, and the sample must be selected. After the data collection tool is selected, the data must be gathered, encoded, analyzed and interpreted.

Even traditional market research is based on the standard quality criteria of quantitative empirical social research. When carrying out a study and analyzing data, researchers must ensure that the results are not distorted by their subjective perceptions, that the collected data are representative and that the conclusions apply not only to the selected sample but to the world beyond. Finally, they must ensure that the generated findings are valid and that the information collected is what the market research project originally set its sights on.

The underlying assumption is that the organization's view of its environment is all the more accurate when customer surveys cover a broader area, customer mentality is analyzed more precisely in focus groups, and competitors are studied in greater depth. If a company does not have the proper view of its environment, it is because it has not yet taken a close enough look.

This metaphor that best captures this mode of understanding is that of a camera that documents the environment as accurately as possible. It is crucial to design a powerful camera and, depending on one's interest, to zoom in on an object as closely as possible or show as much of the object as possible using a wide-angle lens. Invariably, the image of the environment will not be able to provide the promised insights, in which case the "true believers" will claim that the camera was defective, it was held in the wrong way or the object was too far away. There is never any doubt that the "camera" can in principle create an accurate image of the environment.

The traditional view is that an organization's success depends on its ability to accurately evaluate its environment and to closely adapt its own decisions to environmental requirements. A company's success, for example, depends on its ability to precisely anticipate its customers' requests and its competitors' strategies and to respond with its own approaches. Likewise, a political party's success is linked to its ability to meet voter expectations and respond with an appropriate platform. From this perspective, every organization must learn to "adapt to its environment or go under in the struggle against more adaptable rival systems" (Bendixen et al. 1968, 14).

The competitor analysis model developed by Michael E. Porter (1980) offers an "ideal type" of this mode of thinking. According to Porter, in a competitive situation, it is crucial for a company to evaluate various factors in order to be able to optimally position itself in the marketplace. These factors include the threat posed by new market players, the bargaining power of its suppliers, the bargaining power of its customers, the threat of substitutes (i.e. goods that can replace a company's own products) and the intensity of competition. The assumption here is that an organization can objectively grasp its environment. For example, the environment relevant for carmakers—consisting of their customers—is the same regardless of whether it is seen from the perspective of BMW, Mercedes or Audi. Likewise, despite all the segmentation, the electorate is the same for every political party in a country and the rationalities and irrationalities of voters can be accurately determined by electoral research institutes.

## THEORY

### Reflections of the Objectivist Perspective in Organizational Theory

This objectivist view found its way into several early organizational theories. Building in a simplified way on Weber (1976, 562), initial approaches presupposed an "ideal" organization that was based on "precision," "clarity," "documentability," "uniformity" and "rigid subordination." By contrast, a number of more recent organizational theories argue that organizations need to grasp their environmental conditions and structurally align themselves with these "objectively" determined conditions.

In the *contingency approach*, it is assumed that organizations need to adapt to their environment. An organization's degree of specialization, standardization, centralization and formalization depends largely on the competitive conditions, customer structure and technical developments in its environment (see e.g. Pugh/Hickson 1976). Even if, in contrast to the organizational research that draws directly on Frederick Taylor, it is not assumed that there is only one "proper path" for all organizations, this theory is nevertheless characterized by the idea that there is an optimal "fit" between every organization and its specific environment. And, of course, the contingency theory assumes that an organization can objectively grasp environmental conditions.

The *population-ecology* approach to organizational research breaks with instrumentally rational methodologies in that it no longer assumes that organizations can adapt to their environment in a targeted fashion. Ideas about organizational goals vary too widely and information about means-ends relations is too imprecise (see e.g. Hannan/Freeman 1984, 150f.). According to this theory, organizations are generally too sluggish to be able to adapt efficiently to environmental changes. However, random variations constantly lead to the emergence of different types of organizations in the same organizational field. Ultimately, the only organizations that prevail are those that are most closely adapted to their environment. Even if this approach breaks with traditional ideas about the predictability of organizations, it, too, contains the idea that the organizations' environment objectively exists and acts as a selection mechanism in an organizational field.

## 2.2 "Forming"—How Organizations Create Their View of the Environment

Over the last few decades, the assumption of an objectively observable environment has been called into question. We now know not only from biological and psychological research, but also from sociological studies, that every system constantly selects just a few pieces of information from its environment. This limitation is functional: without a filter, the system would collapse from information overload. The highly selective processing of environmental stimuli is a precondition for the system's survival.

The magic word used to describe this phenomenon in systems theory is *autopoiesis* (for a basic discussion, see Luhmann 1986). The term may sound complex, but the underlying idea, which has revolutionized thinking in the natural and social sciences, is relatively simple. Every system—i.e. every microorganism, human being, group and organization—is able to function only in a self-referential fashion. The system's behavior is not determined by environmental events, but results solely from its own structures.

It follows from the concept of autopoiesis that systems are *unable* to "objectively" observe their environment. What a company, public administration, university or a political party sees as its environment is always a construct (Luhmann 2000, 52), which emerges along the lines of "I only see what I believe." Hence, the environment can only be perceived in the way the structures of the system "predetermine" it in all their subjectivity. As Niklas Luhmann pointed out, subjective does not mean arbitrary. A system's subjective conception of the environment must "make sense"—that is, it must enable the system to reduce complexity. Otherwise, the system cannot act in a meaningful, self-sustaining way (Luhmann 2010, 135).

We can use the example of the human brain to illustrate this basic systems-theoretical idea about how perceptions of the environment depend on the system. The brain has no direct contact with its environment. While it is true that environmental stimuli act on the brain (which is "structurally coupled" with its environment), the characteristics of an environmental phenomenon are not depicted in the brain. Rather, the brain uses environmental stimuli to create its own distinct impression of its environment (see Foerster 1996, 137ff.).

Or we can illustrate this idea using example of protest movements (e.g. the environmental and women's rights movements), which naturally assume they are responding to crises that objectively exist in society. However, the very thing that the movements see in society—the threat of nuclear weapons or discriminatory male behavior—is created by the movement's observations. In order to support their own, supposedly objective, view of the environment, these movements collect environmental information about, for example, the nuclear weapons stationed in a country or the percentage of women on supervisory boards, but the point is that the environment is constructed by the observations.

This means that systems produce very different conceptions of their environment without anyone being able to say which ones are objectively correct. Heinz von Foerster illustrated this idea with a story about Pablo Picasso, who was once asked by a visitor why he always painted such abstract pictures and whether he was unable to paint things the way they really are. Picasso responded with a question of his own: "Can you please explain to me what you mean by 'the way things really are'?" The visitor thought for a moment, took a picture out of his wallet and said, "Look, this picture shows my wife the way she really is!" To which Picasso replied, "Oh, your wife is really quite small and very flat!" (see Foerster 1995, 246).

What is the implication of this observation for the question of how organizations perceive their environment?

The essential point is that perceptions of the environment are shaped in important ways by the orientation patterns existing within an organization. It is the "overriding forms of logic," "prevailing scripts," "formative conceptual frameworks," "dominant thought patterns" and "collective mentalities" that determine how the environment is viewed. Or, to put it differently, organizations are only able to draw on those aspects of their environment that their members perceive because of their overriding forms of logic, prevailing scripts, formative conceptual frameworks, dominant thought patterns and collective mentalities.

We call this process of perceiving the environment "forming." In contrast to the passive process of "scanning" the environment, "forming" refers to the active appropriation of an organization-specific view of the environment. Hence, organizations "respond not simply to an existing environment, but to perceptions of the environment that are produced within the organization in a process that is dependent on internal organizational determinations" (Luhmann 2009, 9). Or, to express this thought differently, "The environment influences organizations through the way it is perceived."

## THEORY

### Organizational Theory and the Relationship between "Forming" and "Enactment"

The concept of "forming" is much more fundamental than the idea of "enactment" that is commonly cited in discussions. Richard L. Daft and Karl E. Weick (1984, 287ff.)

argue that organizations can make two different assumptions when they explore the environment and that these assumptions affect the way the environment is perceived. First, organizations can assume that the environment is understandable and measurable. In this case, they play the traditional game of discovering the "correct" interpretation(s). From this perspective, the core process of discovery consists of intelligently collecting, properly measuring and rationally analyzing data. Based on this assumption—and in keeping with an instrumentally rational form of logic—organizations search for unambiguous data and clear solutions. Second, organizations can assume that it is impossible to analyze the environment. In this case, they tend to construct their own environment in a process of enactment. They look for an interpretation that explains past actions and fabricate their own view of the environment. In short, the interpretation of the environment that the organization constructs shapes its view of the environment more strongly than the environment shapes the organization's interpretation.

With the forming concept we radicalize this idea by claiming that every view of the environment is shaped by organizational structures. In other words, if an organization believes its environment is stable and easily comprehensible, it is not because this environment is "objectively" stable and easily comprehensible, but because organizational structures have directed the organization to see the environment as stable and easily comprehensible. As a result of the organization's communication channels, programs and personnel, the organization has adjusted its perceptual patterns such that it convinces itself it has an objective view of the environment, and its actions appear rationally justified.

This process shows that forming is the more general concept through which the structure of an organization predetermines its view of the environment. Drawing on observations by Richard L. Daft and Karl E. Weick (1984, 288f.), we can distinguish a variety of ways in which organizations, in this forming process, perceive their environment. In "conditioned viewing" (1), organizations rely on established instruments to view their environment. The focus is on the routine collection of what are often quantitative data and on deriving appropriate actions from these data, which are seen as objective. In "discovering" (2), organizations assume that their environment can be objectively grasped and assign themselves the task of discovering something new in the environment. For this purpose they use tools from market research, trend analysis and projection calculation to predict the problems and possibilities that they cannot document with the help of "conditioned viewing." In "undirected viewing" (3), organizations assume that their environment cannot be analyzed objectively. On the basis of random information, personal contacts and rumors, they form an opinion about the environment. "Enacting" (4) is a strategy that organizations employ to actively shape their view of the environment. They collect information by trying out new modes of behavior and examining what happens. They experiment, test and simulate, ignoring familiar rules and common expectations.

As part of market exploration, organizations that have used traditional market and trend research methods to engage in conditioned viewing are put in a position to actively shape their view of the environment through enactment processes.

The overriding forms of logic, dominant thought patterns and collective mentalities that determine how the organization perceives its environment result from organizational structures. In organizational research, these structures are defined as decisions that influence a multitude of subsequent decisions. If the retailer Amazon were to ignore a question about working conditions from a journalist from the *New York Times* or the *Washington Post* because these newspapers had criticized working conditions in its distribution centers in the past, it would not qualify as a structural decision. It would only qualify as one if Amazon ignored the question because it had, for example, decided as a matter of principle not to answer any questions from the press concerning working conditions.

Not only do organizational structures—or "decision premises," to use the technical term from organizational theory— substantially restrict the scope of the decisions possible within an organization. They also result in organizations forming a highly selective view. Organizations become highly sensitive to certain phenomena and markedly insensitive to everything else. A Chinese cell phone manufacturer is uninterested in changes to agricultural regulations in Morocco (and has no routine methods to learn about them). A company in the Internet sector has no understanding of the developments on the job market for cleaning personnel (unless it offers cleaning services).

From this perspective, we can see that statements such as "the market demands …," "voters expect …" and "customers want …" are all overly simplistic. It would be more accurate to say "the market demands what a company perceives it to demand because of its structure," "voters expect what political parties project onto them" or "customers want what an organization believes it can offer them." In short, statements about an organization's environment are primarily statements about the organization itself.

## 2.3 The Diversity and Narrowing of Perspectives in Organizations

However, it would be too easy to conclude that, because of their structures, organizations inevitably have a single homogeneous view of their environment. Often the views that different departments, teams and even individuals have of the environment varies considerably within organizations. This has to do with the fact that, due to the very different ways departments, teams and people are integrated into the structure of the organization, they develop their own special thought patterns, mentalities and logic. This means that the view of the environment—i.e. of competitors, customers and partners—is quite different within organizations. Using the language of systems theory, we might say that in any organization, there is not *one* "system-relevant view of the environment" but *many* "system-relevant views of the environment."

One way to understand these different perspectives within organizations is to take a closer look at how departments, teams and people are incorporated into organizational structures. Systems-theoretical organizational research distinguishes three basic types of organizational structures (and describes them in a somewhat complex, yet highly precise way as "decision premises"). The first type consists of the organization's *communication channels*—i.e. the co-signing authority, hierarchical instruction-issuing powers and project networks through which communication is regulated within the organization. An initial, though often distorted, view of communication channels can be gained by examining an organizational chart. The second type of structure is the organization's *programs*—i.e. the decisions made via if-then programs or stipulated targets that can be used to determine whether a member of the organization has acted properly or improperly. The third type of structure consists of *personnel* decisions. This understanding of people as a structural characteristic of organizations can be especially puzzling for business economists, whose thinking is shaped by a conceptual framework that juxtaposes organizational structure (i.e. communication channels) with organizational procedure (i.e. program type). However, it becomes plausible once we consider that personnel turnover often makes other decisions necessary, even if the communication channels and programs do not change. (Luhmann 2000, 279ff.).

These types of structures are perceivable on the different "sides" of the organization. The *formal side* consists of the officially communicated expectations that the organization's members must fulfill to remain in the organization. The *informal side* concerns those expectations that emerge in the shadows of the formal side. They cannot be openly formulated as preconditions for membership, but nevertheless (and for this very reason) have a strong influence on the members' behavior. The *display side* of an organization is its "face to the street"—i.e. those structures that are well suited to serve as the organization's façade vis-à-vis its environment.

Every single division, department, team and even member of an organization is integrated into the organizational structure in a very specific way. A company's sales staff have an important role to play on the display side of the organization, and their interactions with customers are thus managed by means of both formal and informal expectations. The legal department, by contrast, has a different positioning within the organization. Its task is to portray the inevitable "illicit" actions within the organization as lawful in the event of lawsuits. Legal departments are often situated relatively close to top management in the organizational chart and thus have a strong influence on the organization's formal structure.

The organization's perception of its environment is therefore determined not only by *one* overriding form of logic, *one* dominant thought pattern or *one* collective mentality. Rather, within the framework and in the shadows of these dominant views, there emerge competing forms of logic, divergent thought patterns and local views. These are not based on "false perceptions" of the environment (although this is often claimed), but are the inevitable result of the position of the corresponding organizational members within the organizational structure.

An organization's so-called boundary-spanning units are tasked with presenting an idealized image of the organization to

Beyond the Objectivist View—the Cognitive Turn  **35**

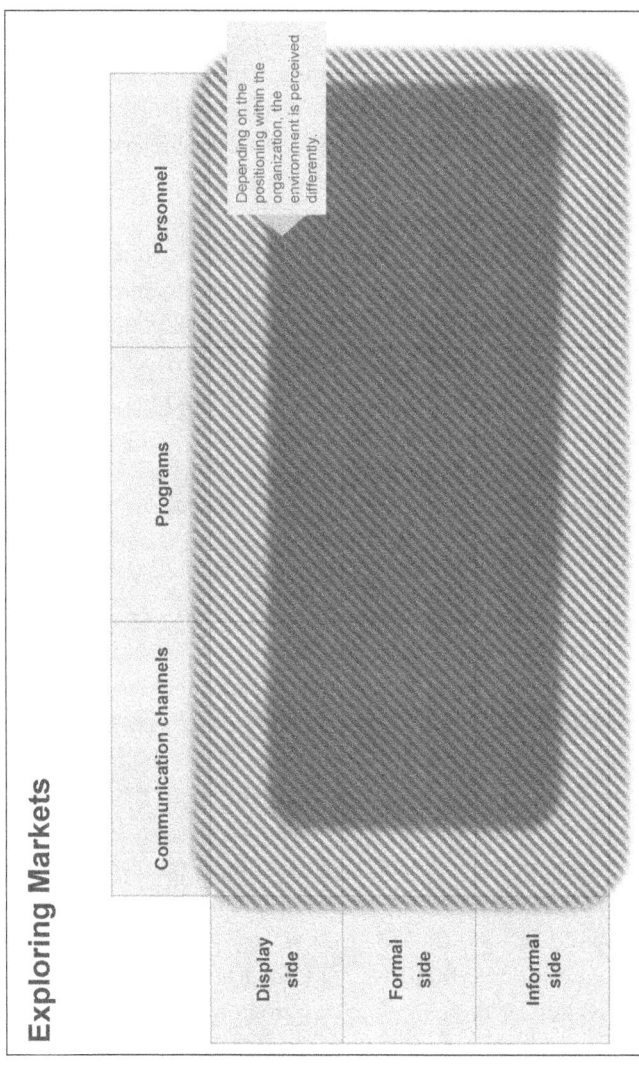

**Graphic 1:** Structural matrix for analyzing organizations

the environment, while at the same time condensing information from the environment so that the organization can process it. The manner in which this information is forwarded by these boundary-spanning units allows for a pre-selection of relevant impressions within the organization (see Adams 1976; Aldrich/Herker 1977). The process results in "front office syndrome," to borrow a term from Richard Cornuelle (1975). Rather than receiving the impressions the environment has of the organizations, the directors of companies, hospitals, armies, public administrations, government departments and political parties receive a view of the environment that reflects the forms of logic, thought patterns and perspectives of front office staff.

By contrast, an organization's so-called technical cores have only highly limited contact with the environment. According to Frederick W. Taylor, the inventor of "scientific management," workers do not need to know anything about the complexity of markets or work processes, but should focus exclusively on processes predefined by experts. The uniformity of many tasks in the technical core results from the fact that surprises and contradictions originating in the environment do not reach the productive core and are instead handled by buffering units (see Thompson 1967, 21). This does not mean that the technical core has no contact with the environment. Indeed, the employees in the technical core often learn through informal channels how customer perceptions are changing and which new political conditions they are facing. But when they share such perceptions, they are often not listened to because the observation of the organization's environment is not part of their formal job description.

From this perspective, it is understandable why debates over assessments of the environment are often so heated. The press department, whose work primarily involves preserving and enhancing the organization's reputation, has a different view of the environment than the purchasing department, which focuses on determining which supplier sells parts at the most favorable price. The quality management department, where customers send their complaints, has a different perspective on the environment than the production department, which receives only sporadic feedback from customers. An individual's position within the organizational structure determines which aspects of the environment he or she observes. The resulting perspectives can come into conflict. This can be useful for the organization because these conflicts can provide a more complex picture of the environment. Additionally, perspectives can exist side by side without employees discussing them. This can also be beneficial for the organization, because all of the employees then work with a coherent picture of the environment and are motivated to act.

> EXAMPLE
>
> **Case Study: The Different Boundary-Spanning Units of Pharmaceutical Companies**
>
> Pharmaceutical companies interact with their partners through special boundary-spanning units. The health policy department works with health insurance companies and medical

associations in order to draw attention to the added value of the company's drugs. The field sales force contacts doctors to provide information on the use of the company's drugs and to ensure higher prescription rates of these drugs. The sales department gets in touch with pharmacists and clinic purchasing departments to negotiate prices.

In this context, it should become clear why a pharmaceutical company's sales department, whose work is characterized by precisely defined targets (goal programs), often has a completely different view of the environment than the quality assurance department, which more closely follows the if-then programs (conditional programs) specified by drug approval authorities.

It is interesting to note that in many cases the different boundary-spanning units of pharmaceutical companies collaborate with the different boundary-spanning units of clinics. Clinic physicians are in contact with the pharmaceutical company's field sales force; hospital purchasing specialists and pharmacists communicate with its distribution and sales department. Clinic directors attempt to influence health policy.

In addition, the different departments in pharmaceutical companies (and also in clinics) interact with each other. However, due to their integration into the organizational structure, they have different perceptions of environmental requirements. At times they may have opposing views, at others they may be in agreement on specific elements.

What is striking, though, is that despite these different, competing perspectives on the environment in organizations, in most cases only one dominant perspective emerges. As a result of micropolitical negotiations, the emergence of fictions about consensus, and the trust placed in the evaluations of the boundary-spanning units, there is often a strikingly homogenous view of the environment in organizations. Members of organizations, argues Karl Weick (1979, 6), often spend considerable time negotiating amongst themselves "an acceptable version of what is going on." Jeffrey Pfeffer and Gerald R. Salancik (1978) refer to the "negotiated environment" of organizations. Slightly modifying this idea, we can speak of "negotiated perspectives on the environment."

Despite the heterogeneity of internal perspectives, organizations often develop, in a self-reinforcing process, a highly selective view of their environment. Because of organizational structures, only a limited cross-section of the environment is taken in. The structures act as filters, allowing only compatible information in, and the organization sees its own view confirmed. On the basis of the information perceived as a result of organizational structures, members of the organization believe in the accuracy of their assessment. The resulting "self-affirmation loop" convinces everyone that their view of the environment is correct.

But there is a more fundamental mechanism behind this self-affirmation loop—the self-fulfilling prophecy. If customers learn that their bank is having payment difficulties, they may withdraw their money in panic. In many cases, this is the very thing that causes the bank to have payment problems in the first place. Managers who have a negative view of employees are unlikely to trust them to take the initiative. They may try to manage staff using narrowly defined rules and guidelines. This can lead to frustration and inner resignation among staff, which can confirm the managers' negative perception of them.

This self-affirmation loop can be observed quite often in companies (see Kühl 2018, forthcoming). One example is the telecommunications division at Siemens, which "slept through" the development of fax machines and data transmission via the Internet. Siemens was one of the first companies to experiment with fax machines and could easily have marketed them, but because it was successful in developing its telex business and learning processes were intensified there, it left the fax business to other enterprises. The same thing occurred in the development of exchanges for telephone networks. Siemens—one of the market leaders in this field—put a great deal of energy into developing switching technology and digitizing its switching centers. Under the catchy name "asynchronous transfer mode," it even came up with a technology that allowed data and voice to be transferred along the same line. Because of the intensive learning efforts in this area, though, management long overlooked the fact that it had become increasingly easier to transmit data and voice over the Internet. Siemens' dominant market position was increasingly jeopardized. The problem, noted former Siemens board member Volker Jung, was that successful products had been promoted far too long. Siemens chronically failed to recognize the shift to new technologies.

A self-reinforcing mechanism in organizations that promotes negotiated perspectives on the environment does not rule out the idea that the competing perspectives in the various organizational departments will continue to exist. From the research on the sudden collapse of companies such as Enron and Lehman Brothers, the last-minute withdrawal of drugs from the market due to side effects, and disasters such as the Challenger crash or the Fukushima nuclear meltdown, we know that in all these cases knowledge existed in individual departments to prevent these events, but this knowledge was unable to prevail against the dominant perspectives in the various organizations.

But what approach can we take to exploring markets? And, more generally, what approach can we take to exploring an organization's environment?

# 3.
# Approaches to Exploration

With the market exploration method, we show how organizations can develop an understanding of their environment. In the market exploration process, it is crucial that the organization's environment be given a "voice"—or, more precisely, "several voices." The goal is not to ask for the opinion of partners from the environment, but to work out these opinions in cooperation with the partners. Customers or suppliers, for example, are often unaware of their own, frequently implicit, assumptions. These assumptions should therefore be analyzed in interactions and then introduced into organizations to provide impetus.

This approach uses various market research methods that are often of a qualitative and not seldom of a quantitative nature. Among the qualitative questioning methods are semi-structured expert interviews, narrative interviews, as well as group discussions with or without visualization aids (e.g. collages, images, organization maps and lifelines). The qualitative observation methods include participant observation, non-participant observation, roleplays and experimentation. The quantitative methods encompass mail, e-mail and Internet questionnaires, live and telephone surveys, as well as so-called prediction markets, where participants bet virtual money on competing ideas. But quantitative observation methods can also be used, such as the collection of behavior-based measurement data by recording app use or by evaluating either street traffic data or the data from barcode-scanning cash registers.

The qualitative methods are based on observing and questioning a relatively small number of participants in order to gain deeper insight into the opinions and behavior of individuals. This approach is especially well suited for discovering something new, understanding complex relations and learning about motivations and intentions. By contrast, the aim of the quantitative methods is to reach a large number of target group members and thus to collect representative answers. This is especially important for determining how widespread a view is in a particular target group. For communication purposes in an organization, the advantage is that, because of their numerical focus, these methods can be presented as producing objectively measured findings and thus provide support for an issue.

The specific feature of the market exploration method (or, more generally, the environment exploration method) is that it discursively combines the different views of the environment shaped by organizational structures and enriches these with perspectives from outside the organization. Through discourse, organizations can explore the scope for action and identify its limits on the basis of the changing organizational view of the environment.

## 3.1. Re-Framing—Changing the Organization's View of the Environment

The structure of an organization creates the "frame" through which that organization takes in its environment. As discussed above, these frames are difficult to fool. They let in the information the organization regards as having a stabilizing effect on its structure. They reject the information that does not suit the organizations' established observation patterns (see Goffman 1974).

In the process of environment exploration, it is important to put oneself in a position to view the environment differently than in the past, or at least to see certain aspects in different ways. For this purpose, organizations need to change features of the frame through which they perceive the environment. "Re-framing"—to use a term introduced from organizational research—is at the heart of this process (see, for example, Bolman/Deal 2008). The challenge is that organizations often have a highly simplified view of their environment. The starting point for re-framing is the questioning of certain aspects of this view. The trick is to give the environment a voice—or, better yet, several voices—and project these voices back into the organization.

The first step is to gain an initial impression of the environment by analyzing studies, literature and both internal and Internet sources. In this way, the exploration history of an organization—consisting of existing data and insights—can be used to create an initial picture. However, it is crucial that the information obtained in this phase be treated with the utmost care. It is often so heavily influenced by the organization's dominant "frame" that it rarely contains surprising insights.

### EXAMPLE

**The Tendency To "Copy and Paste" When Analyzing the Environment of Development Aid Organizations**

Before development banks such as the World Bank, the Asian Development Bank and the EIB grant loans to companies, public administrations and non-governmental organizations in developing countries, they must review these organizations' performance. The objective is to assess whether the organizations will be able to use the loans for investments and pay them back after a grace period.

Normally, the shareholders of these development banks are the governments of the major industrial countries. Because the development banks are forced to prove to these shareholders that they will invest their money in a sustainable fashion, the project managers at the banks must perform credit checks of the borrowers—e.g. water companies, power plants and NGOs.

The problem lies in the difficulty of obtaining a detailed understanding of the borrowers. It is extremely difficult to identify the different interests within organizations. Most power plays take place in secret, and from the outside it is nearly impossible to gain access to informal, trust-based networks.

For this reason, it is common practice in development banks to "copy and paste" when reviewing borrowers. When project

> managers choose to adopt, to varying degrees, the analyses prepared by other banks, they are able not only to save time, but also to build on knowledge that has proved its worth in other projects. These managers are on the safe side because they can point out that "their" analysis is the same as others'.
>
> The problem is that the plausibility of these published and repeatedly copied analyses rests on their similarity. The analyses may enable project managers to meet their banks' internal requirements, but the borrowers remain a black box.

The second step consists of exploratory interviews and observations. In these exploratory interviews, talks are held with actors from the organization's environment. As a rule, these actors are members of organizations whose perspectives are shaped by their own position in their organizations. However, the actors can also include journalists or researchers who observe an organizational field, or even customers who have considered buying a product. An attempt is made in the exploratory interviews to bring to light the interviewees' assumptions, perspectives and motivations. The process can include semi-structured expert interviews based on a catalogue of questions or narrative interviews that use verbal prompts to encourage conversation partners to relate an impromptu story.

The interviews can be supplemented by exploratory observations. This is particularly useful when the goal is to illustrate modes of behavior that cannot be examined in interviews. The conversation partners are often unaware of their behavior or may prefer others not to address it. Frequently, in the exploratory interviews—at least in their initial phase—the "display side" of an organization (or a person) is maintained. In everyday routines, by contrast, this facade is much more difficult to keep up. However, even if something is observed in the exploratory phase, it does not mean participants know the motivation for the observed action.

For this reason, observations and interviews can be combined in exploratory observation interviews. The observation interviews are not conducted in a meeting room, but at the conversation partner's specific place of work or place of consumption. The partner's normal working or conversational routines are not disturbed, but in the course of the observation process, questions are asked about the observed behavior. Because the questions relate to specific actions, it is much more difficult for the conversation partner to keep up his or her facade, and the observer can address modes of behavior that the conversation partner is unaware of, but that are clear to the observer.

The third step consists of peer group discussions in the form of workshops. Because the exploratory interviews are not conducted "from expert to expert" and comparing and contrasting the different views is possible only to a limited extent, it can make sense to bring together several experts at a workshop. What is important here is to maximize the interaction between the participants. Only when different views are contrasted is it possible to gain additional insight besides those already gained in the individual interviews. In this way, the participants' different rationalities can be compared and different explicit and implicit thought patterns can be illustrated.

It can make sense to base these peer group discussions on specific action situations—for example, on the impact of a new legal regulation, the emergence of new technical possibilities or the introduction of new drugs (for an early discussion of the "focusing" of group discussions, see Emory Bogardus 1926, or, of central importance, Morgan 1996). If the discussion focuses on a topic that is relevant to everyone, it is all the more likely that one person's views will be questioned by the others.

The simplest form of the group interview is a heavily moderated recorded discussion that is analyzed afterward. However, group interviews can be initiated and structured by prompts. A frequently used method is the visual representation of the group interview using the Metaplan moderation method or pin board techniques. A overarching structure for the discussion is developed based on a sequence of questions, and contributions are recorded on presentation boards or projected onto a screen with a projector. Another method is a group interview based on organization maps or mind maps. Here the various offshoots and associations triggered by the key concept at the heart of the discussion are represented graphically using a projector. An additional method for group interviews is the timeline, with one group graphically representing and commenting on the development of a phenomenon in chronological order over a longer period. But it is also possible to experiment with the integration of simulation games or role-plays into the group interviews.

Even if the process begins with exploratory interviews, employs, whenever appropriate, observation interviews and concludes with group interviews, it can be useful in individual cases to have the different types of interviews overlap. For example, in individual interviews or observation interviews, participants can more precisely examine insights gained from a group interview. In the process, it can be beneficial to formulate hypotheses about the relations between the exploratory interviews, observation interviews and observations. These hypotheses can help participants gain further insights in the subsequent discussions and further refine questions for the following conversation partners.

## 3.2. "De-Generalization" of Statements

The patterns governing perceptions of the environment are strongly shaped by myths, dogmas and fictions. Myths are handed-down narratives that are no longer scrutinized, dogmas are sets of tenets that we are forbidden to challenge, and fictions are fabrications lacking verification. Myths, dogmas and fictions contain "provable" half-truths, but as a whole they are taken as the truth. People trust their arguments without critically questioning them.

Myths, dogmas and fictions help organizations simplify their view of the environment. In organizational research, they are said to contribute to "absorbing" uncertainty. To borrow a phrase from Albert Hirschman (1967), they produce the ignorance needed to ensure organizations remain capable of action.

A goal of exploration is to gain an understanding of what are often unconscious or barely communicable beliefs—the organization's myths, dogmas and fictions—through a process of de-generalization. In many cases, generalized platitudes are rooted in hidden assumptions, mentalities and motivations. Questions about assumptions, mentalities and motivation are typically answered using knowledge from current management books or with the help of the central points of the last official PowerPoint presentation or general statements such as "That's what the customer wants." This form of generalization must be overcome.

Our *de-generalization* method is a discursive approach to exploratory interviews and group discussions that can be used to bring to light assumptions, mentalities and motivations. In an exploratory interview, conversation partners are first presented with a set of opening questions. They decide where they want to start, but the goal is not to answer all of the questions. The interview is given greater depth using specific action situations, and various options for action are jointly discussed. An initial understanding of the interviewee's assumptions and mentalities emerges.

In group discussions, participants are given the opportunity to review and refine the results of the exploratory interviews. Creating a structure for such group discussions is not always easy. In discussions involving people who are not yet able to judge each other's responses, a censorship mechanism often comes into play. The same applies to discussions involving large groups of people or individuals from outside the organization. Participants do not say everything that comes to mind because they dislike revealing too much about themselves or because they are afraid of boring others. The goal is to overcome this mechanism when moderating the group discussion by ensuring that all supposedly self-evident points are explained, by asking participants to define assumptions in concrete terms and by using specific examples to examine opinions in greater detail.

Ultimately, de-generalization makes use of an approach that has been popularized in the research literature on "high reliability" organizations—i.e. organizations such as aircraft carriers and nuclear power plants that cannot afford to make errors (see Obstfeld et al. 1999 for an extensive discussion in a form suitable for managers). What de-generalization requires and rewards are not abridgements, simplifications or acceleration, but surprising observations, complications and aggressively communicated contradictions.

### EXAMPLE

#### Liberated from the Dogma of Guidelines

A pharmaceutical company that specialized in the fight against cancer saw potential for its drugs, which were used to prevent side effects in chemotherapy. A study found that oncologists prescribed this company's supporting therapy much less frequently than was recommended by international treatment guidelines. The company believed that it needed to demonstrate to physicians that they were not complying with these guidelines. This information alone would lead to a broader use of the supporting therapy and thus substantially increase sales of the company's drugs. The thinking went like this: "Guidelines must be followed because they are based on interpretations of studies by an international body of experts."

In exploratory interviews with physicians, though, it soon became clear why medical staff often undermined the guidelines in their daily work, without openly opposing them. The physicians considered the risk of side effects in chemotherapies to be overestimated, and they questioned whether, for certain types of cancer, the supporting therapy made sense at all. They had their own rationale for when to use the supporting therapy, independent of the guidelines. They prescribed it when side effects had been observed in the pre-therapy phase or if an outpatient lived too far away from the treatment center for potential side effects to be detected at an early stage. In other cases, the treatment was not used.

What was important in the peer group discussion with oncologists was to show the pharmaceutical company's staff that their strategy of citing guidelines was not very promising. The goal was to shed light on the physicians' reasons and arguments for rejecting the guidelines, which had been identified in the de-generalization phase. This was essential to make clear to staff why the physicians did not base their decisions on the guidelines and why their minds would not be changed by studies focusing on insufficient guideline compliance. The pharmaceutical company had to abandon this argument and rethink its marketing strategy.

## 3.3. Hypotheses Formation— Articulating Assumptions in Order to Make Progress with Exploration

As discussed above, when the environment of an organization is explored, it is never possible to obtain all the available information. It is only possible to make preliminary assumptions about how things are now or how they will be in the future. Often this is done unconsciously. The aim of exploration is to take participants through this process of formulating and testing assumptions in controlled form. The assumptions about the environment—we call them "hypotheses"—are explicitly articulated. Such hypotheses in the form of articulated sentences are assumed to have a preliminary validity, which is then discussed.

Hypothesis formulation begins early on in environment exploration. In the exploratory interviews and group discussions, observations are made and striking statements are noted down. Participants ask how their conversation partners' behavior can be explained and why they behave as they do. The first hypotheses are formulated on the basis of this discussion. Participants question what needs to be analyzed further in order to confirm the hypotheses or to offer opposing views. On the basis of the hypotheses, questions are formulated for use in follow-up conversations and individual interviews, and participants consider whom they need to speak to next. The hypotheses are thus refined in talks with the actors and are used specifically as the basis for the next interactions.

# 4.
# Options for Constructing Reality—Conclusion

Let us assume that organizations do not objectively scan existing environmental conditions, but construct their environment themselves. If our assumption is correct, there is an ideal way to change the organizations' view of their environment—change organizational structures. As shown above, this can be done by modifying communication channels, by eliminating old programs and introducing new ones, and by hiring, firing or transferring personnel.

On the level of *communication channels*, organizations can change the way they construct reality by, for example, establishing additional departments (e.g. for contacts with shareholders or non-governmental organizations) and thus by opening up a new perspective on the environment. Or they can change the way they perceive their environment by introducing a fundamentally new organizational structure—much like the large US companies that have switched to divisional structures with special profit centers.

On the *program* level, organizations can change their view of the environment by varying their program structure. Conditional programs cause the organization to pay close attention to a triggering impulse in the environment. Goal programs focus the organization's attention on the achievement of objectives—especially when they are linked to additional monetary incentives.

If goal or conditional programs are changed, it always results in changes in the way the environment is perceived. Due to its conditional programming, a fire department, for example, responds reflexively to emergency calls. Because of this focus on a trigger, it pays only limited attention to fire prevention. If prevention is important to the fire department, it must set up its own goal program in order to take this environmental factor into account.

On the *personnel* level, organizations can influence the way they perceive the environment by firing, hiring or transferring employees. When a company or an industry association appoints a state secretary to its board, it may be motivated not only by an interest in influencing politics, but also by a desire to establish special "sensors" for political developments via the new board member's former contacts. To cite another example, the policy of poaching personnel from non-governmental organizations—which is currently widespread in the chemical, pharmaceutical and energy industries—is driven at least in part by the desire to anticipate critical objections from protest movements.

But even if there are various ways for organizations to use decisions about their formal structure to influence their view of the environment, this should not fool anyone into thinking that the way the environment is perceived is a process that is easy to control. Not only does the painstakingly constructed "display side" of the organization perform important functions in presenting a polished image of the organization to the outside world. It also shapes the way organizations perceive their environment. And an organization's informal structure—the undecided decision premises—often exerts an even stronger influence on the scripts, conceptual frameworks and thought patterns that govern the organization's view of its environment.

Creating environmental conditions is often a hard-to-control process. Management has only a limited capacity to define which environmental factor is considered relevant within the organization. Managerial measures such as benchmarking against organizations from the same or from different organizational fields, implementing traditional market research measures, and using qualitatively based market exploration processes are attempts to systematize this process. The challenge lies in creating new observational perspectives for the organization with the help of a temporary process—perspectives that, due to their loose connection to organizational structure, cannot be immediately rejected by the organization's immune system.

# Bibliography

Adams, John S. 1976. "The Structure and Dynamics of Behavior in Organizational Boundary Roles." In *Handbook of Industrial and Organizational Psychology*, edited by Marvin D. Dunnette, 1175–99. Chicago: Rand McNally

Aldrich, Howard E., and Diane Herker. 1977. "Boundary Spanning Roles and Organization Structure." *Academy of Management Review* 2:217–30.

Bendixen, Peter, Eberhard Schnelle, and Wolfgang H. Staehle. 1968. *Evolution des Management*. Quickborn: Verlag Schnelle.

Bogardus, Emory S. 1926. "The Group Interview." *Journal of Applied Sociology* 10:372–82.

Bolman, Lee G., and Terrence E. Deal. 2008. *Reframing Organizations: Artistry, Choices, and Leadership*. 4th ed. San Francisco: Jossey-Bass.

Cornuelle, Richard C. 1975. *De-Managing America: The Final Revolution*. New York: Random House.

Daft, Richard L., and Karl E. Weick. 1984. "Toward a Model of Organizations as Interpretation Systems." *Academy of Management Review* 9:284–95.

DiMaggio, Paul J., and Walter W. Powell. 1983. "The Iron Cage Revisited: Institutional Isomorphism and Collective Rationality in Organizational Fields." *American Sociological Review* 48: 147–60.

Evan, William M. 1966. "The Organization-Set: Toward a Theory of Interorganizational Relations." In *Approaches to Orga-

*nizational Design*, edited by James D. Thompson, 318–27. Pittsburgh: University of Pittsburgh Press.

Foerster, Heinz von. 1995. "Worte." In *Weltbilder – Bildwelten*, edited by Klaus Peter Dencker, 236–46. Hamburg: Hans-Bredow-Institut.

Foerster, Heinz von. 1996. "Erkenntnistheorien und Selbstorganisation." In *Der Diskurs des radikalen Konstruktivismus*. 7th ed. edited by Siegfried J. Schmidt, 133–58. Frankfurt a.M.: Suhrkamp.

Goffman, Erving. 1974. *Frame Analysis: An Essay on the Organization of Experience*. New York: Harper & Row.

Hall, Robert E. 2002. *The Response of Prices to Shifts in Demand*. Stanford: Stanford Working Paper.

Hannan, Michael T., and John Freeman. 1984. "Structural Inertia and Organizational Change." In *American Sociological Review* 49:149–64.

Heidenreich, Martin, and Gert Schmidt. 1992. *Informatisierung, Arbeitsorganisation und Organisationskultur: Eine vergleichende Analyse der Einführung von Informationssystemen in italienischen, französischen und deutschen Unternehmen*. Bielefeld: FSP "Zukunft der Arbeit."

Hirschman, Albert O. 1967. *Development Projects Observed*. Washington, D.C.: The Bookings Institution.

Kühl, Stefan. 2009. "Capacity Development as the Model for Development Aid Organizations." In *Development and Change* 40:551–77.

Kühl, Stefan. 2013. *Organizations: A Systems Approach*. Farnham: Gower.

Kühl, Stefan. 2018 (forthcoming). *The Rainmaker Effect: Contradictions of the Learning Organization*. Princeton/Hamburg/

Shanghai/Singapore/Versailles/Zurich: Organizational Dialogue Press.

Lant, Theresa K., and Joel A.C. Baum. 1995. "Cognitive Sources of Socially Constructed Competitive Groups." In *The Institutional Construction of Organizations*, edited by W. Richard Scott and Soren Christensen, 15–38. Thousand Oaks: Sage.

Luhmann, Niklas. 1986. "The Autopoiesis of Social Systems." In *Sociocybernetic Paradoxes: Observation, Control and Evolution of Self Steering Systems*, edited by Felix Geyer and Johannes van der Zouwen, 172–92. London: Sage.

Luhmann, Niklas. 1990. "Risiko und Gefahr." In *Soziologische Aufklärung*, edited by Niklas Luhmann, 131–69. Opladen: WDV.

Luhmann, Niklas. 1991. *Soziologie des Risikos*. Berlin/New York: Walter de Gruyter.

Luhmann, Niklas. 1995. *Social Systems*. Stanford: Stanford University Press.

Luhmann, Niklas. 2000. *Organisation und Entscheidung*. Opladen: WDV.

Luhmann, Niklas. 2009. "Zur Komplexität von Entscheidungssituationen." *Soziale Systeme* 15:3–35.

Luhmann, Niklas. 2010. *Politische Soziologie*. Frankfurt a.M.: Suhrkamp.

Morgan, David L. 1996. "Focus Groups." *Annual Review of Sociology* 22:129–52.

Obstfeld, David, Kathleen M. Sutcliffe, and Karl. E. Weick. 1999. "Organizing for High Reliability: Processes of Collective Mindfulness." *Research in Organizational Behavior* 21:81–123.

Pfeffer, Jeffrey, and Gerald R. Salancik. 1978. *The External Control of Organizations: A Resource Dependence Perspective.* New York: Harper & Row.

Porter, Michael E. 1980. *Competetive Strategy: Techniques for Analyzing Industries and Competitors.* New York: Free Press.

Pugh, Derek S., and David J. Hickson. 1976. *Organizational Structure in its Context: The Aston Programme*, vol. 1. Westmead/Farnborough: Saxon House.

Smircich, Linda, and Charles Stubbart. 1985. "Strategic Management in an Enacted World." *Academy of Management Review* 10:724–36.

Suthoff, Karl. 1960. "Marktforschung und Gesellschaftsstruktur." *Markenartikel* 22:86–88.

Thompson, James D. 1967. *Organizations in Action.* New York: McGraw-Hill.

Varoufakis, Yanis. 2012. *Der globale Minotaurus: Amerika und die Zukunft der Weltwirtschaft.* München: Kunstmann.

Weber, Max. 1976. *Wirtschaft und Gesellschaft.* Tübingen: J.C.B. Mohr.

Weick, Karl E. 1979. *The Social Psychology of Organizing.* New York: Random House.

White, Harrison C. 1981. "Where Do Markets Come From?" *American Journal of Sociology* 87:517–47.

www.ingramcontent.com/pod-product-compliance
Lightning Source LLC
Chambersburg PA
CBHW020303030426
42336CB00010B/888